BRITAIN IN PICTURES

THE BRITISH PEOPLE IN PICTURES

BRITISH HISTORIANS

GENERAL EDITOR
W. J. TURNER

★

The Editor is most grateful to all those who have
so kindly helped in the selection of illustrations,
especially to officials of the various public
Museums, Libraries and Galleries, and
to all others who have generously
allowed pictures and MSS.
to be reproduced.

BRITISH HISTORIANS

E. L. WOODWARD

WITH
8 PLATES IN COLOUR
AND
21 ILLUSTRATIONS IN
BLACK & WHITE

WILLIAM COLLINS OF LONDON
MCMXXXXIII

PRODUCED BY
ADPRINT LIMITED LONDON

★

PRINTED
IN GREAT BRITAIN BY
WM. COLLINS SONS AND CO. LTD. GLASGOW

Ald Gate

LIST OF ILLUSTRATIONS

PLATES IN COLOUR

BLACK & WHITE ILLUSTRATIONS

'KING EUGENIUS OF SCOTLAND CAUSES
HIS ANCESTORS' HISTORIES TO BE WRITTEN'
Woodcut from Holinshed's *Chronicles*, 1577

I

IT would be pleasant to begin this survey with a phrase about a certain "island" temperament manifesting itself over the centuries in the work of British historians. An "island" temperament. "English" is not an inclusive term : "British" to a historian means primarily the island of Great Britain, to the northern limit of Roman domination, before the coming of the Anglo-Saxon and Scandinavian invaders. There is, however, no need to quarrel about terms. Bede (672-3—735) the earliest, and, in many respects the greatest of the "island" historians, wrote an *Ecclesiastical History of the English Nation*. This book was written in Latin, and at a time when the "English Nation" had no unified political existence. Bede himself was the subject of a Northumbrian king whose rule extended, across the later Anglo-Scottish border, from the Firth of Forth to the Humber. More than a thousand years later another *History of England* became a best-seller ; the author was David Hume, a Scotsman from Berwickshire. About half way in time between Bede and Hume, Gerald de Barri, a Welshman of Norman ancestry, compiled the first "full-length" geographical description of Ireland. The honours may therefore be taken as even.

To some extent, indeed, it is possible to notice a difference, age for age, between English (for short) and continental historians. Bede, once again, is typical of the average "English" scholar. A certain quietness of mind ; a strong visual imagination ; a clear style, not without poetic quality ; a shrewd, tolerant judgment ;

7

greater interest in character and action than in ideas. Among the readers of these "English" historians perhaps one might find a stronger dislike of pedantry and "dry-as-dust" than is found in some other countries. Nevertheless, the field of English historical writing is too vast to be summed up in a few sentences, and the individuality of the writers too stubborn to be juggled into averages. Macaulay had not a "quiet manner"; Stubbs had little visual imagination. Carlyle's judgment was not "tolerant." Gibbon's style cannot be described as "poetic." Neither Hume nor Acton was uninterested in ideas.

Furthermore, as the centuries have passed, the balance and emphasis of historical studies and writing have changed so much that there might seem to be little in common between the medieval chroniclers, the encyclopedists of the eighteenth century, and the "economic-minded" historians of the present day. It is well to remember that, as there has always been some kind of special technique, so also has there been a distinction between historians whose main interest is in the establishment of fact, and historians who have concerned themselves with the significance of the facts thus established. A little more than a hundred years ago, Macaulay, in his large and vivid language, wrote of the "two hostile elements," reason and imagination, which had "never been known to form a perfect amalgamation" in history. "Of the two kinds of composition into which history has been thus divided, the one may be compared to a map, the other to a painted landscape. The picture, though it places the country before us, does not enable us to ascertain with accuracy the dimensions, the distances, and the angles. The map . . . presents no scene to the imagination; but it gives us exact information as to the bearings of the various points, and is a more useful companion to the traveller or the general than the painted landscape could be."

Is it possible, then, to divide British historians into "map-makers" and "landscape-painters"? During the last four centuries there have been successive waves of protest against the overweighting of detail in history, and successive demands for a distinction between fact and "significant" fact, but the definition of "significant fact" has varied from generation to generation, and the division between annalists and philosophical historians has never been clear-cut. One might add that Macaulay lived before the age of aerial photography, and that a good map is a more exciting thing than a bad landscape painting.

It is better to look for special marks of British historical writing in another direction. Historians in Great Britain have been interested in subjects which have also interested their European contemporaries. They have written in the language and style of their times; Latin, Norman French, Elizabethan English, English of the Augustan age or of the Romantic Revival. They have passed judgments according to the standards of their environment. They have also been influenced by the events of English history and by the slow accumulation of circumstances in which English habits and English ways of thought have taken their national form and particular shape.

The people of this island have no claim to any special endowment of moral virtue; their history does not shew an unbroken continuity, still less a monopoly,

O felica ôfcula Lactenuf labuf impisa. al
inter ctefua indiena tepranuf inf.... nete
uirpate vie gt te fili invi illusbret...... cu
nevuf gt parte 3t ôi genit impatre.

ACMATHIAS PARISENSIS

THE VIRGIN AND CHILD WITH MATTHEW PARIS KNEELING BELOW
Illumination by Matthew Paris from his Shorter History

SIR WALTER RALEIGH 1552?–1618
Oil painting by Hubert L. Smith

in the moral exercise of political and economic power. Nevertheless, for the last three hundred years, their national experience has given to them a sense of limits, a belief in liberty and toleration, and a practical conviction that the misuse of power brings retribution in the temporal sphere. The transition from medieval to modern times in politics and religion, and in the general social order, was made with less violence and bloodshed in this island than in almost any other part of the western world. Great Britain has known a longer period of internal peace and freedom from invasion than any country on the European mainland. She has met, and defeated, tyrannies which have threatened or overwhelmed country after country. Her own insular situation and dependence upon sea power have taught her, after one bitter lesson in the eighteenth century, the dangers of provoking a great maritime coalition against her navy. This tale of fortunate accident could be prolonged to cover many other aspects of British national life. For example, the custom, legally established, that the younger sons of the nobility rank as commoners has saved us from the deep cleavage between the *noblesse* and the third estate which long barred the way to internal unity in France.

It is thus to be expected that British historians, who, by definition, are concerned with the past, would have learned the large lessons of British history. They learned these lessons at an early stage. It is sometimes thought that the "moral approach" to history, the notion that the abuse of power brings retribution in this world, is a particularly Victorian feature of political and historical thought. Yet this idea, which, incidentally, dominated the historical writing of the Greeks, is strongly developed in Milton. It is found also in the eighteenth century. The cool and sceptical Gibbon could write : "I shall not, I trust, be accused of superstition, but I must remark that, even in this world, the natural order of events will sometimes afford the strong appearance of moral retribution."

The "moral approach" to a study of the "natural order of events" has its dangers, although the historian may be well aware that moral ideas have a history. Take two minor instances. In the nineteenth century Stubbs was not the only historian whose belief in the bracing effect of representative institutions led him into too great an emphasis upon the importance of parliamentary assemblies in the English middle ages. Freeman misunderstood many features of the eleventh century because he saw the lineaments of Mr. Gladstone in the West Saxon Earl Godwin. Nevertheless, if the "moral approach" may lead to distorted and unhistorical judgments, it can also give to a historian sympathy and elevation in his treatment of the past. Froude, for example, was a man of strong prejudices on the side of protestantism. Yet, as a prelude to the religious struggle between catholics and protestants, Froude could write :

"Here therefore we are to enter upon one of the grand scenes of history ; a solemn battle fought to the death, yet fought without ferocity by the champions of rival principles. Heroic men had fallen, and were still fast falling for what was called heresy ; and now those who had inflicted death on others were called upon to bear the same witness to their own sincerity. England became the theatre of a war between two armies of martyrs to be waged not

9

upon the open field in open action, but on the stake and on the scaffold with the nobler weapons of passive endurance. . . . . If we would understand the true spirit of the time we must regard Catholics and Protestants as gallant soldiers whose deaths, when they fall, are not painful but glorious, and whose devotion we are equally able to admire even where we cannot equally approve their cause."

The "moral approach" of English historians has led to self-criticism as well as to sympathy. English historians have condemned the treatment of Ireland by their fellow-countrymen in the eighteenth and nineteenth centuries far more severely than Prussian historians have dealt with the Prussian treatment of Poland since the time of Frederick the Great.

II

THESE judgments upon the misuse of power have been made, for the most part, by men who have had some practical experience of affairs. In order to understand the tradition of British historical writing it is necessary to remember that the "academic" historian, the "professor of history" is a recent figure. There have been Historiographers Royal (there is still a Historiographer Royal for Scotland), but in the development of historical writing their office has counted no more than the office of Poet Laureate in the development of English poetry. Until 1724, Great Britain had no professors of "modern" history. In this year George II founded the Regius Chairs at Oxford and Cambridge. These foundations had a practical purpose ; the training of diplomats. The professors were expected to supervise the instruction of undergraduates in modern languages. For a century the holders of the chairs were of little importance in the growth of historical studies. As late as 1841 Thomas Arnold saw nothing incongruous in holding the chair of modern history at Oxford (where, incidentally, he lectured on Roman history) while he was headmaster of Rugby.

British historians have thus been learned scholars, but, until our grandfathers' times, few have done their best work, or even any of their work, as professors. This fact is important. Guizot once said that, until he had taken part in government and administration, he had underrated the genius of Napoleon. Clarendon put this same point of view more sharply :

"It is not a collection of records or an admission to the view and perusal of the most secret letters and acts of state that can enable a man to write a history, if there be an absence of that genius and spirit and soul of an historian which is contracted by the knowledge and course and method of business, and by conversation and familiarity in the inside of courts, and with the most active and eminent persons in the government."

The scope of history is wider to-day than in the seventeenth century. Familiarity with the inside of courts is no longer a necessary part of a historian's equipment. Some kind of practical experience is necessary, and it is remarkable how many of

BEDE 672-3—735
Engraving from André Thevet's *Portraits et Vies des Hommes Illustres*, 1584

the greatest British historians have had this experience. Bede lived in the monastery of Jarrow at a time when the joint abbeys of Jarrow and Wearmouth were centres of northern culture. Matthew Paris, a monk in the important abbey of St. Alban's, was known personally to King Henry III and was sent on a mission of state to Norway. Sir Walter Raleigh, Clarendon, and Macaulay were concerned with the most important affairs of state. Burnet was chaplain to William of Orange on his expedition to England, and throughout his life was active in public affairs. Hume went, as a minor but not obscure figure, on several diplomatic missions. Gibbon was a captain in the Hampshire militia before he wrote his history, and a member of parliament (holding, for a time, a place under the Crown) while he was writing his earlier volumes; he has told us that "the captain of the Hampshire Grenadiers was not useless to the historian of the Roman Empire."

11

In the nineteenth century, Grote was a banker, Arnold a headmaster, J. R. Green the vicar of a London parish ; Acton was busy with politics and journalism, Bryce with politics and diplomacy. A good many holders of academic chairs to-day acquired, twenty-five years ago, first hand experience of "the discipline and evolution of a modern battle." Finally, it will not be forgotten that the historian of Marlborough is now Prime Minister of Great Britain.

One might extend this survey to the antiquaries in order to shew that, in Great Britain, the study of the past has not meant exclusion from present activities. The great Camden was in turn second master and headmaster of Westminster. Moreover, the collection of historical material and the writing of history have been encouraged or enjoined by kings and statesmen for practical reasons ; reasons one might say, of dignity of state as well as of policy. King Alfred ordered and took part in the translation of Bede's *Ecclesiastical History*. He was also responsible for the development, and, probably, for the first compilation of the *Anglo-Saxon Chronicle*, a record almost unique in Europe, and continued, after Alfred's time, until the twelfth century. Later, after many generations, Archbishop Parker in Elizabeth's reign made a collection of manuscripts in order to establish the continuity of the Elizabethan church with the medieval past. This collection included the most important of the manuscripts available to-day for students of Alfred's chronicle.

Archbishop Parker's practical motives were shared by many of the historians and antiquaries of the seventeenth century. One of the typically English features of the civil and religious conflicts of this century was the appeal, not to abstract notions of right, but to historic precedents. Hence there were solid and immediate reasons for the investigation of the past, although these reasons did not of themselves lead to impartial writing. It is, however, dangerous to attribute any single motive to historians. The same writer may well combine disinterested curiosity with extreme partisanship ; "the care of knowing causes", in the seventeenth century phrase of Thomas Hobbes, is as great as the pleasure of getting the last word in an argument. There is the simplest motive of all for the writing and study of history : the appeal of tragedy as a purging of the emotions of pity and terror.

> "Let us sit upon the ground
> And tell sad stories of the death of kings."

There is also a practical motive, not connected with political or ecclesiastical advocacy, but directly associated with personal conduct. Men have written histories because they have thought, not without justification, that, if history does not repeat itself, historical situations recur, and that directly useful lessons can be learned from the past. Sir Walter Raleigh believed that the purpose of history was "to teach by example of times past such wisdom as may guide our desires and actions." Nearly a century and a half later Lord Bolingbroke repeated this view in the epigram that history is "philosophy teaching by example." Once again, after an interval of more than a hundred years, S. R. Gardiner, the most careful and unprejudiced of historians, wrote that he wanted to convey "something better than information . . . It seems to me that, without any attempt at preaching, merely to explain how men acted towards one another, and the reason of their misunderstandings ought to teach us something for the conduct of our lives."

Acton's whole career shewed that he held this view, and that he too combined it with an absolute impartiality in scientific judgment. In our own time when "preaching," direct or indirect, is out of fashion, the "moral approach" to history, in the sense of a warning against private as well as public abuse of power, is implicit in the *saeva indignatio* with which scholars like Dr. and Mrs. Hammond have approached the social and economic history of the early nineteenth century.

Whatever the motives of historians, the field of historical curiosity has widened. There were more people in England during the lifetime of Oliver Cromwell than in the reign of Alfred; they were doing a greater variety of things. There were many more millions in the nineteenth century; they were doing an even greater variety of things. Moreover in the course of the generations the quality as well as the quantity of written records has increased. Before the age of printing few people in western society could read or write; outside the learned professions there was not a vast amount of business for which reading and writing were essential. The continual increase in the complexity of affairs since the fourteenth and fifteenth centuries has brought a greater demand for accuracy in the records of public and private transactions. Consider for example, the task of balancing the national accounts in an age before the introduction of arabic numerals or the invention of double-entry book-keeping. In the twentieth century the accumulation of "known facts"—precisely, not approximately known facts—has set the historian a problem hardly known to earlier ages. The trouble now is not the finding of material, but the selection of "significant fact" from a mass of *data*.

DETAIL FROM THE TITLE PAGE OF MATTHEW PARIS'S *GREATER CHRONICLE*
Edition of Archbishop Parker, 1571

ILLUMINATION FROM GEOFFREY DE MONMOUTH'S *HISTORY OF BRITAIN*
Early 14th century

III

IT is necessary to remember the limiting conditions of the time in dealing with the work of medieval historians. These historians were chroniclers. They wrote down the story of events; they took for granted the social and economic background. Many of the happenings which interested medieval men, and particularly, medieval churchmen, have little detailed interest to-day. Nevertheless, for those who will take trouble to get some knowledge of the background, and to read medieval chronicles in their proper context, there is plenty of excitement. The context is, however, remote; the antique and, often, child-like setting in which the work was done sets barriers to unfamiliar readers. Until the thirteenth century medieval chronicles tend to be bare records strung together in poor Latin. Most of them were written in monasteries, for the good reason that there were few places outside the monasteries where historical study was possible. The interest, or rather, the bias of the chroniclers was often ecclesiastical in the narrowest sense; respect for the rights of a particular monastic order, or for the property of one monastic house became the standard by which kings and even popes were judged. Nevertheless a monastery, and especially one of the greater monasteries situated on a much travelled road, was a good centre for historical writing, and the nearest medieval equivalent to a modern news agency. A large community, with widely scattered properties, and with interests touching and touched by affairs of state; a community affiliated to other houses of a single order, and reaching across the seas to the court of Rome; a guest-house receiving travellers of every rank and station, and collecting the talk of the realm.

Bede, like most men of genius, is the great exception to generalisations about the aridity of the early historians. Bede had a clear, logical, encyclopedic mind;

14

THE ELEPHANT SENT BY ST. LOUIS TO HENRY III IN 1255
Illumination from Matthew Paris's *Historia Major*

he knew how to control his material, and how to write. Incidentally, any one who dates a letter to-day is following Bede's method. Bede introduced, though he did not invent, the style of reckoning years from the year of the Incarnation. From Northumbria this calculation of "years of grace" was brought, probably by the Devonshire man Boniface, to the Frankish court, and thence to the papal Curia.

There were indeed other writers whose work deserves the title of history ; for example, William of Malmesbury (c.1080-c.1143), a monk of Anglo-French descent who wisely modelled himself on Bede, or the Yorkshireman, William of Newburgh (d. c. 1198) whose political judgment and insight were unusual for his age. Matthew of Paris, English by birth, in spite of his designation, is the most interesting of the historians of the thirteenth century. Matthew Paris entered St. Alban's abbey in 1217. He went to Norway in 1248 as the bearer of a message from Louis IX of France (St. Louis) to King Haakon VI of Norway. The King of Norway invited him to reform the Benedictine abbey at Trondjhem. After carrying out this work, Matthew Paris went back to St. Alban's, and lived there

15

until his death in 1259. St. Alban's already had a competent school of historians ; Matthew Paris continued their chronicle of events. He wrote in a pleasant, easy style, but he was less scrupulous than Bede, and not above tampering with the text of documents (including the text of Magna Carta). His interests were narrow and his judgments often those of a partisan, yet he was bold enough to write down criticisms of the king's policy. It is true that he did not intend these criticisms to see daylight ; he noted in the margin against the more doubtful passages of his work the Latin word *offendiculum* ; a little offence.

IV

MATTHEW PARIS wrote in Latin because his readers expected serious history to be written in Latin. There were indeed in the later middle ages a number of rhyming chronicles in English, but these jingles can hardly be called histories, though they are neither more nor less readable than the first crabbed prose compilations in the English tongue. The English prose chronicles of the sixteenth century told the Elizabethans all that they knew about the earlier history of England and Scotland. Raphael Holinshed (d. c.1580), for example, one of the latest in a long sequence, gave Shakespeare the plots for most of his historical plays. Holinshed worked as a translator in the printing office of one Reginald Wolfe. Wolfe had already planned a universal history and cosmography ; Holinshed helped him to carry out this enterprise. Wolfe died before the work was finished. Holinshed then limited it to a history of England, Scotland and Ireland.

The vernacular chroniclers were laymen. They wrote for a lay public. They were not irreligious laymen, uninterested in church affairs, but their interests, and those of the new class in English society which read their books, were not bound up with an oecumenical church. They wrote, also, in an age of rapid social and political change. Historians to-day are a little wary about the use of the term "renaissance." The middle ages were not a period of intellectual stagnation; there were at least two "revivals of learning" between 800 and 1300. The so-called "new learning" of the fifteenth and sixteenth centuries was not altogether new, even as learning. In any case, the reception of the new ideas was slow and uneven ; one might describe the seventeenth century as a period of greater intellectual importance and originality than the Tudor period.

On the other hand there is much truth in the view that the age between the death of Richard III and the accession of James I saw a general widening of secular intellectual interests, and the establishment of a new class in a central and dominating position in English society. Medieval conditions were not unfavourable to speculative and artistic genius, but there is a quality about men like Sir Thomas More and Sir Walter Raleigh which had been almost unknown in western Europe since the end of the Roman peace. These men were not "modern" ; they were the grandsons and great-grandsons of medieval men. Nevertheless, for better or worse,

MACBETH AND THE THREE WITCHES
Woodcut from Holinshed's *Chronicles of England, Scotlande and Irelande*, 1577

our own "modern" ideas, our secular outlook, our scientific culture reach back directly to the years in which Greek and Latin authors were read in a new way, and scholars and artists recovered a lost continuity with the ancient world.

The significance of this age can be seen in English historical writing. Sir Thomas More wrote a *History of King Richard III*. This work is not a piece of modern historical research, but it is nearer in style, in delineation of character, and in maturity of judgment to a work of the present age than to a medieval chronicle. Consider this summary of the character of Richard III :

> "Free was hee called of dyspense, and sommewhat above his power liberall. With large giftes hee get him unstedfaste frendeshippe, for which hee was fain to pil and spoyle in other places, and get him stedfast hatred. Hee was close and secrete, a deepe dissimuler, lowlye of countenaunce, arrogant of heart, outwardly coumpinable where he inwardely hated, not letting [*i.e.* hesitating] to kisse whome he thought to kyll, dispitious and cruell, not for evill will alway, but after for ambition, and either for the surete and encrease of his estate. Frende and foo was muche what indifferent where his advauntage grew. He spared no man's deathe whose life withstoode his purpose."

Here is the Richard III whom Shakespeare put into his play, but the man was already drawn for him.

"History hath triumphed over time." This sentence in Sir Walter Raleigh's *History of the World* sums up at once the magnificence and the secular outlook of the Elizabethan age. Raleigh's words have a tragic meaning because the *History of the World* was written while the author was detained in the Tower under sentence

17

of high treason. Others, possibly Ben Jonson, helped him in certain parts of the book, but the whole work bears the impression of a man who, above all others, added grace to everything which he touched. Raleigh planned to write a general history until the island of Great Britain began to take an important part in world affairs ; thenceforward the book would concentrate upon the history of England, though Raleigh intended to allow himself digressions or, in his military language, "sallies." He began with the Creation; one of his "sallies" discusses, with much learning and practical observation from his own travels, whether the tree of knowledge was the Indian fig-tree, and whether Adam and Eve clothed themselves with the commodious leaves of this tree.

Raleigh had always been a great reader ; he had taken a trunk of books with him on every voyage. Obviously, even with his learning and reading he could not compile, at second hand, a history of the world from the beginning of historical legends ; he never reached the Christian era. In any case, his book was in danger of suppression because James I thought him "too saucy" in his treatment of princes. James was touchy on this subject, but Raleigh went a little far for the age when he wrote of Henry VIII that "if all the pictures and patterns of a merciless prince were lost in the world, they might all again be painted to the life out of the story of this king."

To the moſte hygh and

vertuous Princeſſe, MARY by the grace of GOD, quene of
Englande, Spayne, Fraunce, both Sicilles, Ieruſalem, and Ireland, defen-
dour of the fayth, Archeducheſſe of Auſtria, Ducheſſe of Burgondy,
Myllayne, and Brabant, Counteſſe of Haſpurge, Flaunders, and
Tyroll, her highneſſe moſte humble and obedient ſubiect,
VVyllyam Raſtell ſeriant at lawe , wiſſheth health,
wealth, honour, and felicitie, worldely and
euerlaſtyngly.

DEDICATION TO QUEEN MARY I
From Thomas More's *Works*, 1557

TITLE PAGE OF RALEIGH'S *HISTORY OF THE WORLD*
First edition, 1614

V

RALEIGH'S history shews, incidentally, two features of the age which are reflected in most of the contemporary historical works; an interest in oceanic exploration and in the study of English antiquities. Here again the novelty lies as much in the approach to the subject as in the content of the works. There were travel-books and studies of ancient lore and traditions in the middle ages, but there is far more than a difference in date of publication between Geoffrey of Monmouth's twelfth century *History of British Kings* and Sir Henry Spelman's work on the Councils of the English Church or between the compilation of tall stories put together under the title of Sir John Mandeville's *Travels* and Hakluyt's *Voyages and Discoveries.*

Richard Hakluyt (1553-1616) was a scholar whose interest in geography and sea-voyages began with his first sight of a map of the world. He lectured for a time on geography at Oxford, and was for five years chaplain to the English Ambassador in Paris, but the greatest of his works was written while he was rector of a Suffolk parish.

His three volume work (the full title is *The Principal Navigations, Voyages, Traffiques and Discoveries of the English Nation made by Sea or over Land to the Remote and Farthest Distant Quarters of the Earth*) describes in a discursive way more than two hundred voyages. Although Hakluyt took a good many seamen's stories on trust, he also added to his collection numbers of documents, charters, letters of privilege and the like. Moreover he had a patriotic intention in writing his book. He wanted England to be the greatest sea power in the world; he was providing the "significant facts" which might help towards the attainment of this end. Hakluyt had "heard in speech, and read in books other nations miraculously extolled for their discoveries and notable enterprises by sea, but the English of all others for their sluggish security, and continual neglect of the like attempts." His book is an answer to this charge, whether made against his countrymen in times past or in his own age. The answer is summed up in the proud sentences of his "Epistle Dedicatorie":

> "Which of the kings of this land before her Majesty, had theyr banners ever seene in the Caspian sea ? which of them hath ever dealt with the Emperor of Persia, as her Majesty heth done, and obteined for her merchants large and loving privileges ? who ever saw before this regiment, an English Ligier in the stately porch of the Grand Signor at Constantinople ? who ever found English Consuls and Agents at Tripolis in Syria, at Aleppo, at Babylon, at Balsara, and which is more, who ever heard of Englishmen at Goa before now ? what English shippes did heeretofore ever anker in the mighty river of Plate ? passe and repasse the unpassable (in former opinion) straight of Magellan, range along the coast of Chili . . . travers the mighty bredth of the South sea, . . . enter into alliance, amity, and traffike with the princes of the Moluccaes, and the Isle of Java, double the famous Cape of Bona Speranza, . . . and last of al returne home most richly laden with the commodities of China, as the subjects of this now florishing monarchy have done ?"

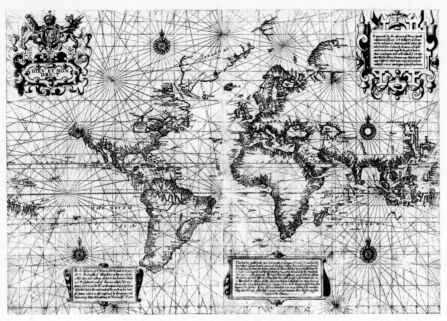

CHART OF THE WORLD
From Hakluyt's *Voyages and Discoveries*, 1598

John Stow, one of the antiquaries of the age, wrote that "the searching and unsatisfied spirits of the English" had led them to these voyages of discovery. It might be said that there were similar motives in the minds of the antiquaries themselves, but these men had another reason at least for the collection of historical material. The dissolution of the monasteries had brought the dispersal of many great and small libraries. The content of medieval knowledge was as much out of fashion as the theology of the eighteenth and early nineteenth centuries is out of fashion to-day. The old books and manuscripts were often thrown away as so much rubbish; John Bale (1495-1563), a Carmelite friar who turned protestant, and became bishop of Ossory, described the attitude of many (though not of all) of those who acquired monastic buildings:

> "A number of them which purchased these superstitious mansions reserved of those library books some to serve their jakes, some to scour their candlesticks, and some to rub their boots, and some they sold to the grocers and soap-sellers, and some they sent overseas to the bookbinders, not in small numbers, but at times whole ships full. Yea, the universities are not all clear in this detestable fact."

The monastic buildings were in many cases treated as badly as the manuscripts. It is therefore to the honour of the antiquaries of the later sixteenth and seventeenth centuries that they did what they could to leave a record of the visible monuments

21

THE TOWER OF LONDON
Engraving from John Stow's *Survey of London and Westminster*. First published 1598

of medieval England. One of the earliest of these antiquaries, John Leland (c. 1505-1552 was chaplain, librarian, and antiquary to Henry VIII. Calais was at this time within the king's realm, and therefore within the territorial boundaries of Henry's "great alteration in the state ecclesiastical." The king gave Leland the living of Poppeling near Calais, but allowed him to appoint a deputy while he made a six years' tour of England. Leland's *Itinerary* (which was not printed until 1710) was the result of this "laboriouse Journey and Serche for England's Antiquities." One of Leland's letters throws an interesting light on the continuity of national habits. Leland asked that the books from the monastic libraries should be preserved in the King's Library. This measure "would be a great profit to students, and honour to this nation ; whereas now the Germans, perceiving our desidiousness and negligence, do send daily young scholars hither, that spoileth them [*i.e.* the books], and cutteth them out of Libraries, returning home and putting them abroad as monuments of their own country."

John Stow (c. 1525-1605), a London tailor, also made journeys on foot over many parts of England in order to examine historical manuscripts. As far as his purse allowed, he bought old books and manuscripts to save them from destruction. Archbishop Parker helped him with patronage and money ; after Parker's death, Stow's resources were smaller, yet he gave up all his time to research and writing. He published a *Survey of London* in 1598. It is to the discredit of the "new learning" that, in his old age, Stow had to ask for a royal license to "repair to churches, or other places, to receive the gratuities and charitable benevolence of well-disposed people," and that, notwithstanding, he died in want.

Hic oculos similes vultusq; hic ora tueri
Poteris, nec vltra hæc artifex quiuit manus.

ANNALES ipsum, celebrisq BRITANNIA monstrant
Perenniora Saxo et ære μνήματα.

Quisquis et Historiæ Cathedram hanc conscenderit, esto
Benignitatis vsq monumentum Loquax.

DEGOREVS WHEAR PRIM⁖
HIST·PR·P·E·POSVYT

Marcus Gheeraedts pinxit

WILLIAM CAMDEN 1551-1623
Oil painting by Gheeraedts (?)

Stow's younger contemporary William Camden (1551-1623), was more fortunate
in his circumstances, though his great work *Britannia* was written while he was a
schoolmaster.   He travelled a good deal in the school holidays, visiting ancient sites
and monuments.   In 1597 he was given one of the heralds' offices, and was thus
more free to spend time on antiquarian research.

23

Leland, Stow, and Camden were interested mainly in the materials of history : manuscripts, buildings, archaeological remains, ancient sites. Sir Henry Spelman, a Norfolk gentleman, was one of the first scholars to study, in an ordered way, the early history of English institutions. Leland had taught himself Anglo-Saxon. Spelman made investigations into the language, and published a glossary of obsolete terms in the laws of England.

<h2 style="text-align:center">VI</h2>

T HESE antiquaries began an age of massive learning, which, as ever, was not free from pedantry and "collector's mania." The reaction of the ordinary reader in favour of "significant fact" goes back to the sixteenth century. Sir Philip Sidney in his *Apologie for Poetrie* (c. 1581) sets out the claims of a poet, a moral philosopher and a historian. The historian is introduced in unflattering terms as "loden with old mouse-eaten records, authorising himselfe (for the most part) upon other histories, whose greatest authorities are built upon the notable foundation of Heare-say, . . . better acquainted with a thousand yeeres a goe than with the present age: and yet better knowing how this world goeth then how his own wit runneth : curious for antiquities, and inquisitive of novelties, a wonder to young folkes, and a tyrant in table talke."

Although the demand for something more than a *précis* of "mouse-eaten records" was met slowly, the seventeenth century produced at least two short works of synthesis by writers of genius. One of the two is Bacon's *History of the Reign of King Henry VII*. Bacon remarked wisely and deeply on the study and writing of history in his *Advancement of Learning*. His short biography is not more than a compilation, but it is written in Bacon's laconic and masterful style, and ends with a portrait of the king which later research has done little to change. For example :

> "The less Bloud hee drew, the more hee tooke of Treasure. And (as some construed it) hee was the more sparing in the One that hee might bee the more pressing in the Other ; for both would have beene intolerable."

Or, again, one sentence sums up this grim sovereign :

> "For his Pleasures, there is no Newes of them."

Milton's *History of Britain, that Part especially now called England ; continued to the Norman Conquest* is the first account of England before 1066 put together by a great artist. Milton was more critical than the Elizabethan compilers. He set little store on the early writers through whose work "the indistinct noise of many Battels and Devastations of many Kingdoms, overrun and lost, hath come to our Eares." He thought it useless to give too much time to the "Civil Broils" of the eighth century, and made no secret of his contempt for the "antiquitarians" who took "pleasure to be all thir lifetime in raketing the Foundations of old Abbies and Cathedrals" :

> "I am sensible how wearisom it may likely be to read of so many bare and reasonless Actions, so many names of Kings one after another, acting little

EDWARD GIBBON 1737–1794

Oil painting by Henry Walton

'THE DEATH OF NELSON'

From the wall painting in the Houses of Parliament by Daniel Maclise, 1806–1870

more than mute persons in a Scene : what would it be to have inserted the long Bead-Roll of Archbishops, Bishops, Abbots, Abbesses, and thir doeings . . . swelling my Authors each to a voluminous body, by me studiously omitted ; and left as thir propriety, who have a mind to write the Ecclesiastical matters of those Ages ; neither do I care to wrincle the smoothness of History with rugged names of places unknown, better harped at in *Camden* and other Chorographers."

Milton's history is worth reading because Milton wrote it. The greatest historical work of the seventeenth century was, however, a record, not of the remote and legendary past, but of contemporary events. Bacon had suggested that the "writing of Lives" should be more frequent. Clarendon's *History of the Rebellion and Civil Wars in England* is an autobiography on a grand scale. Edward Hyde, earl of Clarendon, was the son of a country gentleman of fair standing. He made his way at the bar and soon became a figure in the literary and political society of London. At the outbreak of the civil war Hyde joined Charles I. He went into exile with Charles II, and, before the Restoration, became the King's Lord Chancellor. From the Restoration in 1660 until 1667 he was the King's chief minister. After his fall from power he lived in France. Here he finished the history which he had begun in an earlier exile. The *History* is indeed a composite work. Clarendon began to write in 1646 ; he had not intended to publish his book. He was writing only for the King, and for a few chosen statesmen in order that they might learn the mistakes which had lost the royalist cause, and the policy by which the kingdom could be regained for the monarchy.

For twenty years Clarendon's book was unfinished. When he went into exile in 1667 he could not take his papers with him. Therefore he decided once again to write a history of his time, and to write it for his family as an autobiography. In 1671 his son was allowed to visit him, and to bring him his papers. Clarendon then resolved that, after all, he would write a history which in due time might be published. For this purpose he combined the earlier private history with the autobiography, and added the necessary connecting chapters.

The great achievement of Clarendon is not in narrative (though his descriptions are vivid and interesting) but in the full portraiture of character. Clarendon was a partisan, yet he could be just, according to his time, to his enemies. In his own way he was just to Oliver Cromwell :

"Without doubt no Man with more wickedness ever attempted anything . . . yet wickedness as great as his could never have accomplished those designs without the assistance of a great Spirit, an admirable circumspection, and sagacity, and a most magnanimous resolution. . . . In a word, as he was guilty of many Crimes against which Damnation is denounced, and for which Hell-fire is prepared, so he had some good qualities which have caused the Memory of some Men in all Ages to be celebrated ; and he will be looked upon by Posterity as a brave, wicked Man."

On the other hand Clarendon was not blind to the faults of Charles I :

"His Kingly Virtues had some mixture and allay that hindred them from shining in full Lustre, and from producing those fruits they should have been attended with . . . He was very fearless in his Person ; but, in his riper years, not very Enterprising. He had an excellent understanding, but was not confident enough of it... To conclude, He was the worthiest Gentleman, the best Master, the best Friend, the best Husband, the best Father, and the best Christian that the Age in which he lived produced. And if he were not the greatest King, if he were without some parts and qualities which have made some kings great and happy, no other Prince was ever unhappy who was possessed of half his Virtues and Endowments, and so much without any kind of Vice."

The noblest of Clarendon's portraits is that of Lord Falkland who was killed in the first battle of Newbury. Falkland was only 33 at the time of his death. Until the outbreak of the civil war "his condition of life was so happy that it was hardly capable of improvement." His house at Great Tew, within riding distance of Oxford, was a centre of learning and wit ; his friends thought as highly of his judgment as of his ability. Falkland supported the king, but could not support him with the simple loyalty of a soldier like Sir Edmund Verney who summed up his attitude in the words : "I have eaten the king's bread, and served him now thirty years, and I will not do so base a thing as to desert him."

To Falkland's more subtle and reflecting mind the mere fact of civil war was a matter of deep melancholy. "From the entrance into this unnatural War his natural chearfulness and vivacity grew clouded, and a kind of sadness and dejection of spirit stole upon him, which he had never been used to." In the morning of his last battle "as allways upon action, he was very chearful," but, as the months had passed, he had become strangely morose and severe.

"When there was any Overture or hope of Peace, he would be more erect and vigorous, and exceedingly solicitous to press anything which he thought might promote it ; and, sitting among his friends, often after a deep silence, and frequent sighs, would, with a shrill and sad accent, ingeminate the word *Peace, Peace ;* and would passionately profess 'that the very agony of the War, and the view of the calamities and desolation the kingdom did, and must endure, took his sleep from him, and would shortly break his heart.' This made some think, or pretend to think 'that he was so much enamoured on Peace that he would have been glad that the king should have bought it at any price,' which was a most unreasonable Calumny."

There were men on each side in the civil war who hated violence, and yet agreed with Falkland that peace could not be "bought at any price." On the parliamentary side the best contemporary history illustrating the ideas of the puritans was written by a woman. Mrs. Lucy Hutchinson, daughter of Sir Allan Apsley, Lieutenant of the Tower, wrote a life of her husband, Colonel Hutchinson. She wrote only for her own family, and her book was not published until 1806. For readers in the early nineteenth century Mrs. Hutchinson shewed the puritans in a new light. Hitherto, for all their private virtues, they had been regarded as philistines and boors, with Milton as a curious exception. Mrs. Hutchinson was something of a *grande dame*, and the circle in which she moved was very far from that of the non-conformist society of an English provincial town in the early years of the nineteenth century.

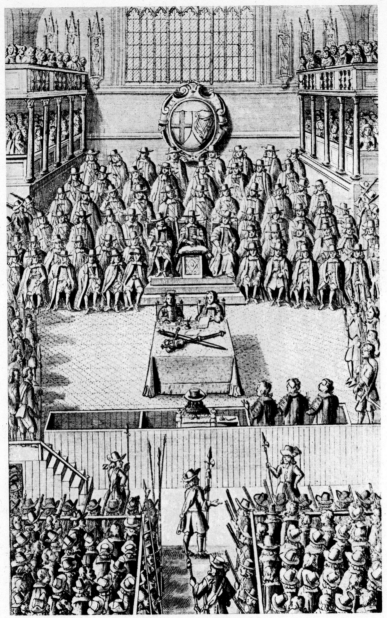

TRIAL OF CHARLES I, 1649
Contemporary engraving

Modern research has brought into the foreground of history many other private papers and memoirs of the period of the civil war, but, for a modern reader, Mrs. Hutchinson's book is probably more interesting than other and longer works of a more political or polemical kind.

Gilbert Burnet, the last of the contemporary historians of the seventeenth century (Pepys and Evelyn were diarists, not historians) was, like Clarendon, though on a lesser scale, an actor in the events which he described. Burnet was born in Edinburgh, and graduated in Aberdeen. He was for a time professor of divinity at Glasgow, but settled in London in 1674. Here he gained a reputation as a preacher, and here also he published the first two volumes of his *History of the Reformation of the Church of England*. Burnet might have had a bishopric, if he had cared for court favour, and if he had not written a strong letter of remonstrance to the king on his "sinful pleasures" as well as on the evils of his government. After the accession of James II, Burnet, who had already travelled abroad, lived at the Hague, and became one of the principal advisers of William of Orange. William rewarded him in due course with the bishopric of Salisbury. In his later years Burnet wrote a *History of My Own Time*. The first volume of this work was not published until 1724; the second volume appeared ten years later. Burnet's times were then out of fashion, and the history was not well received. It is true that Burnet was self-important, prejudiced, and a little gullible about facts, yet he tried to be fair and accurate. Nevertheless his way of writing did not please the age. Swift, who disliked Burnet's politics, said of the book that he had "never read so ill a style." A modern generation is more likely to be satisfied with Burnet's quick and plain-spoken English, and less likely to feel offence at his political partisanship.

VII

IF the age of Pope and Swift was too sophisticated to enjoy Burnet, the learned tomes of the antiquaries were equally out of fashion. There had not been wanting a succession of scholars to continue the work of Leland, Camden, and Spelman. Sir William Dugdale (1605-1686) had begun during the Protectorate the publication of the English monastic charters, and had also written a book on the *Antiquities of Warwickshire*. Thomas Madox (1666-1727) wrote a learned history of the Exchequer. Thomas Rymer (1641-1713) historiographer to William III, put together, with the help of Robert Sanderson, a collection in twenty volumes of English treaties. Rymer was more successful as a collector of historical material than as a dramatist and dramatic critic. His *Foedera* survived as a standard work of reference. His historical play, *Edgar*, has been forgotten, and his *Tragedies of the Last Age Considered* will be remembered, if at all, for his unfavourable judgment upon the plays of Shakespeare.

Rymer's absurd literary judgment explains a good deal of the neglect, and indeed contempt, in which these scholars were regarded by their more brilliant if less

WILLIAM DUGDALE 1605-1686
Frontispiece to Dugdale's *History of St. Paul's Cathedral in London,* 1658

learned contemporaries. English medieval scholarship of the late seventeenth and early eighteenth centuries has not been rescued from this undeserved contempt until our own generation. The scholars of the time (they included at least one woman : Elizabeth Elstob, who wrote an Anglo-Saxon grammar) did much to develop the methods of critical study, or, one might say, the method of history as a science. Their learning was, in a literal sense, monumental. They had an obstinacy, and often a noble passion, for truth ; they knew that the truth about the past cannot be found without hard and often dull work. They also knew that a great deal of the "history" written by men of letters is pleasant reading, but nearer to fiction than to "significant fact." Hearne, one of the oddest of the antiquaries, once put this point in a letter to a friend:

> "We must consider how very little history there is : I mean real authentick history. That certain kings reigned, and certain battles were fought we can depend upon is true : but all the colouring, all the philosophy of history is conjecture."

If the critical methods laid down by these scholars had not been undervalued in England, if the material which they collected had been put to use, there would have been no need for Englishmen to learn over again from Germans the scientific treatment of texts. Even so, the antiquaries set an example in the study of local history in which England was pre-eminent in the eighteenth century. (An observer wishing to correlate the development of learning with contemporary social conditions would notice that county history had a special appeal to county families.) Unfortunately these scholars and antiquaries were, for the most part, tiresome, unpractical, pernickety men, without much skill in writing, or ability to see the wood for the trees. They frightened away the ordinary reader ; they bored the finished and elegant writers of the age even more than the table talk of their predecessors had bored Sir Philip Sidney.

This boredom was repaid by a cool and, at times, impudent disdain. Lord Bolingbroke, in his *Letters on the Study and Use of History* (1735), reviewed the utility and achievements of the patient servants of scholarship and research as a landed magnate might have reviewed the lesser figures of his household establishment. He admitted that it was difficult "to avow a thorough contempt for the whole business of these learned lives" ; the obligation to such persons, in every branch of scholarship, would be greater "if they were in general able to do anything better, and submitted to this drudgery for the sake of the public." Lord Bolingbroke recommended a "temperate curiosity" about the past :

> " Some [histories] are to be read, some are to be studied, and some may be neglected entirely, not only without detriment, but with advantage. Some are the proper objects of one man's curiosity, some of another's, and some of all men's ; but all history is not an object of curiosity for any man. He who improperly, wantonly, and absurdly makes it so, indulges a sort of canine appetite ; the curiosity of the one, like the hunger of the other devours ravenously and without distinction, whatever falls in its way."

The generation to which Lord Bolingbroke belonged was unlikely to produce a great historian. Furthermore, while in the seventeenth century there were practical reasons for searching the political and ecclesiastical annals of the past, in the middle years of the eighteenth century the establishment of state and church seemed fairly secure. In any case, until Burke once again appealed to history against the claims of an abstract political philosophy, the easy and comfortable doctrines of Locke satisfied men's minds. There was no need to dig up precedents from the years of

RIDDLE'S CLOSE, EDINBURGH, WHERE HUME LIVED FOR A TIME
Engraving from Daniel Wilson's *Edinburgh in the Olden Times*, 1848

"gothic" barbarism. Indeed, as Lord Chesterfield told his son, "much time would be ill-employed in a minute attention" to the history of the five or six centuries after Charlemagne.

Nevertheless, all English history, if not all history, remained "an object of curiosity" to the reading public, and, in the middle and later years of the eighteenth century, there was an increasing demand for "complete" histories of Great Britain. Once more the economic and social changes of the age were bringing new classes of readers, and greater opportunity for reading. Houses were better heated in winter, candles gave a brighter and steadier light. Chairs and living rooms were more comfortable, libraries more humane. Books could be printed more cheaply, sold and advertised more widely as communications improved, and newspapers had a larger circulation.

The scholars of "intemperate curiosity," who would not play down to the public, cared nothing for this great new market. Hence the demand for complete histories was met at first by writers whose knowledge was unequal to their task. One of the earliest forerunners of the modern popular history was Thomas Carte's four-volume *History of England to 1654*. Carte had the misfortune to lose most of his subscribers after the appearance of his first volume in 1747 because he made the mistake of saying that he had met someone who had been cured of the "king's evil" by the Old Pretender. In any event, Carte was little more than a hard-working compiler who would have lost his market to any competitor of first-class ability.

This market was taken by two Scotsmen, David Hume (1711-1776) and William Robertson (1721-1793). A third Scotsman, Tobias Smollett, better known as the author of *Roderick Random* and *Humphrey Clinker*, also wrote a *Complete History of England*; other Scots collaborated with an Englishman, George Sale, and a Frenchman, Georges Psalmanazar, in the production of a *Universal History* of gigantic dimensions. Sale was a remarkable man; a Kentish solicitor with a real interest in oriental scholarship. He published a translation of the Koran in 1734, and took part in the revision of the Arabic New Testament produced by the Society for the Promotion of Christian Knowledge. Psalmanazar was a more flamboyant figure who deceived the learned world for some time by pretending to be a native of Formosa; he backed his claim by an invented Formosan alphabet and grammar. After his fraud had been exposed, he became very pious and won the respect of Dr. Johnson. The *Universal History* was not the only work of its kind. A similar venture, on a smaller scale, was launched with a preface by Oliver Goldsmith, for which the writer was paid the sum of three guineas.

Fifty or more volumes of world history suited some tastes in this age of encyclopedias. Other readers wanted less dispendious tomes, and were more curious about England than about the rest of the world. For this more limited demand Goldsmith himself wrote a four-volume history of England. The book would not be worth remembering if Goldsmith had not been the author, and if he had not disarmed criticism by the charming apology that he had written "not to add to historical knowledge, but to contract it."

VIII

DAVID HUME turned to history almost by chance, and after the greater part of his philosophical work had been done. He had applied without success for philosophical chairs at Edinburgh and Glasgow. In 1752 he was appointed Keeper of the Advocates Library at Edinburgh. Here he decided to make

'THE BURGHERS OF CALAIS'

A typical 19th century historical illustration
From Darton's Children's Picture Series

THOMAS BABINGTON MACAULAY 1800–1859
Oil painting by Sir Francis Grant

use of his access to original and secondary historical sources : that is to say, sources already in print. Hume did not propose to bother himself with manuscripts and other unprinted sources. Within two years he produced a first volume of a *History of England*. The volume covered the reigns of James I and Charles I. (It is of interest that, in the nineteenth century S. R. Gardiner spent about thirty years in dealing with the same period.) Hume's first volume was not a popular success. The author was so much disappointed that he thought of leaving Scotland, changing his name, and settling in France. The outbreak of war with France made this plan impracticable. Hume therefore went on with his book. The sale of the second volume justified the addition of two volumes on the Tudors and two on the earlier period from Julius Caesar to the accession of Henry VII.

These volumes had an immense number of readers. Hume set a new standard of historical writing. He raised history to a philosophical plane, and clarified it of an excess of detail. He wrote in an easy, flowing style, although Dr. Johnson (not forgetting his dislike of Scotsmen) complained that the structure of his sentences was French. Lord Bolingbroke and other writers of his time had inclined to reduce history to a case book for statemen or a manual of examples for young men about to take part in affairs. Hume knew the difference between "fact" and "significant fact"; he also knew that the significance of history lay in the widest interpretation of human action rather than in any discrete series of "lessons." Hume's own interpretation was indeed very far from complete. He followed his age in a dislike of "enthusiasm," and in a preference for settled government, even though it might be arbitrary government. He cared more for order than for liberty, and was not much interested in "improvement." He overlooked almost entirely the importance of religion. A friend gives the reason : "Early in life he had conceived an antipathy to the Calvinistic divines." Nevertheless, in spite of his superficiality and his cocksureness, Hume does give his readers an idea of the unity of history, at all events in the sense of a cyclical progress in human affairs. A cyclical progress ; there was no finality about it, no long-sustained achievement. In Hume's own words, "there is a point of depression as well as of exaltation, from which human affairs naturally return in a contrary direction, and beyond which they seldom pass, either in their advancement or decline." All the more reason, therefore, to be gratified that one had the good fortune to be born into an advanced and civilised epoch like the eighteenth century.

Hume was a great historical writer, but he was not a great historian. His "significant" facts were not always accurate facts. He took his material almost entirely from the secondary sources in his library, and owed a good deal to the industry of the unlucky Mr. Carte. Hume's "intellect was perhaps too active and original to submit with sufficient patience to the preparatory toils and long-suspended judgment of a historian." So wrote a critic in the next generation. One might say, perhaps, more shortly, that Hume did not take enough trouble.

William Robertson was one of the Calvinistic divines whom Hume, in general, disliked. Robertson published in 1759 a *History of Scotland during the Reigns of Queen Mary and of King James VI till his Accession to the Crown of England.* This book also became an immediate success, and, for his next historical work, a *History of the Reign of Charles V*, Robertson received the princely and unprecedented sum of £4,500. He then turned to subjects outside Europe, and produced a *History of America* and a *Historical Disquisition on Ancient India*. The range of Robertson's work also shews its limitations. On the other hand, Robertson's merits were like those of Hume, though on a lesser scale. A lucid, even, prose style, burdened, in Robertson's case, with too many heavy Latinisms ; an "elegant" arrangement of fact ; suitable philosophical reflections. The facts were taken at second hand ; the reflections were a little commonplace, and most modern readers would agree with Cowper's description of the style as "pomp and strut."

The influence of Hume and Robertson can be seen in the writings of a host of lesser imitators who gave the public what the public wanted, and did well out of their work. Robert Henry (1718-1790) deserves to be remembered where others are forgotten because he was one of the earliest historians to write a "social history." Dr. Johnson once said that he wished much " to see one branch of history well done, that is, the history of manners, of common life." Hume had included in his work a small survey on these lines. Henry's *History of England on a New Plan* limited the narrative of political history to one section in each of his six volumes. The other sections dealt with the constitution and laws, religion, learning, the arts, and the state of manners.

These writers of popular works, attesting an astonishing demand, were eclipsed by the genius of Edward Gibbon. Gibbon was born in Putney in the year 1737. His *Autobiography* describes with *aplomb* the main facts about his life. He may have dramatised his decision to write the history of the decline and fall of the city of Rome when he says that he made up his mind on the subject as he "sat musing on the Capitol, while the barefooted fryars were chanting their litanies in the temple of Jupiter." The setting fits exactly with his summary of his own work ; "I have described the triumph of barbarism and of religion."

The choice of subject, which Gibbon soon expanded to include the fall of the Roman Empire, may well be called a decision of the whole man. Gibbon had indeed always been interested in historical subjects, and had long been considering a theme upon which to write a *magnum opus*. The growth of Swiss liberties, a biography of Sir Walter Raleigh, a comparison, on Plutarchian lines, between the Emperor Titus and King Henry V had been among these projects. Gibbon actually wrote a short work on the liberties of Switzerland : the biography of Sir Walter Raleigh would have been a curious affair, but it was never even begun. Even after his decision to take the immense theme of the Roman Empire, Gibbon waited before engaging upon his subject. He did not begin to write until about 1772 ; his first volume appeared in 1776, his last in 1788.

The Decline and Fall of the Roman Empire is unique not merely in English historical writing, but in the historical writing of any country. No work of such length has maintained its popularity for so long a time. As a modern critic has pointed out, Gibbon's book is "constantly republished with notes and additions as though it were an original authority." No history can survive, except as a source of

MEXICAN HISTORICAL PICTOGRAPH
Frontispiece to William Robertson's *History of America*, 1777

material for experts, unless it is also a work of art. The *Decline and Fall* is a great work of art ; it is not a work of the purest or noblest art, since Gibbon was an un-heroic figure living in an unheroic age. Nevertheless, if he were incapable of great emotion, Gibbon was a master of "passionless impartiality" towards all men and things below the heroic level. This mastery is one of the main sources of his power. He was not an original thinker ; his scholarship was not extraordinary, though it is significant that he was among the few "literary" historians who did not underrate the work of the antiquaries. He acknowledged his debt to others, and, in particular, to the French historian Tillemont. He failed—the failure was universal long after Gibbon's death—to do justice to the services rendered to civilisation by the Byzan-tine Empire. He knew little about the western middle ages. "The triumph of barbarism and religion" ignores the existence of countervailing facts over which modern scholars have spent years of investigation. It ignores equally the triumph of Chartres Cathedral, of the philosophy of St. Thomas, and of the *Divine Comedy*. Finally, the lack of nobility in Gibbon's work is a little too obvious, and there is

35

something repellent about his *obscénité érudite et froide*. When all this has been said, Gibbon's achievement remains in the forefront of English historical writing. For the first time in any European language a single work, covering a period of more than a thousand years, was carried through from beginning to end without ever losing itself in digressions and side issues. Nothing is redundant or inconsistent ; every chapter and every page fit perfectly into the general scheme. No great ship was ever launched more smoothly. Hume had judged events in a long sequence, and had lifted their narration to a higher level. Gibbon had a finer visual imagination as well as a greater care for accuracy of fact. He wrote in a mandarin style, inimitable, uniform, heavy, artificial ; yet the repetition of the same cadences, the same measurement of words, the same antithesis of sentences does not become wearisome. The book can be read ; the book is read, and, centuries hence, readers will continue to savour Gibbon as they savour Dr. Johnson.

IX

GIBBON died in 1794. For nearly twenty years after his death almost the only historical work of importance published in England was Sharon Turner's *History of England from the earliest period to the Norman Conquest*. Sharon Turner was a lawyer by profession. He settled in 1795 in the neighbourhood of the British Museum because he wanted to be near to the manuscripts in the library. It is significant, though not surprising, that Sharon Turner's work has been forgotten by the general public, and that little attention was ever paid to it except by other scholars. A generation later Palgrave's *Rise and Progress of the English Commonwealth* hardly met with a better fate. Palgrave's book did not extend beyond the rise of the commonwealth ; even this story was left incomplete, though in a later work Palgrave reached the Norman Conquest. These books were not widely read because they were in fact unreadable. The public, as always, wanted history ; the scholars gave them historical research. As Sir Walter Scott pointed out in the preface to the 1829 edition of the Waverley novels, "when the author addresses himself exclusively to the Antiquary, he must be content to be dismissed by the general reader with the comment of Mungo, in the *Padlock*, on the Mauritanian music, 'What signifies me hear, if me no understand ?' "

At first sight the situation appears to be similar to that of the early eighteenth century. There were, however, several changes of such magnitude that an analogy between the two periods is misleading. In one respect it is possible to find continuity. In the early nineteenth century, as in the age of Lord Bolingbroke, the universities gave little thought to the history of England or, for that matter, to the modern history of Europe. This neglect was more striking, and, for a time, more serious because the universities on the continent of Europe, and particularly in Germany, were paying notable attention to historical studies ; though here again it must be remembered that the main impulse to the study of national history came from outside academic circles. The development of these studies in Germany was

THE CAPITOL FROM THE SIDE OF THE CENTRAL STEPS
Engraving by Piranesi, dated 1776

due in part to political motives, but there was a solid basis of scholarship upon which this political superstructure could be built. German scholars had done remarkable work in the field of philology, in the editing of texts, and in the study of law. This work was directed at first to classical texts and to ancient history; the new methods were soon extended to other spheres. This extension, in turn, was partly, though not wholly, the result of the Romantic Revival. The first stages of the Romantic Revival were literary ; a search for new forms and new subjects at a time when the so-called classical modes of the eighteenth century were becoming stale, cold, and hackneyed. The search for the glamour of "far-off things" was most easily satisfied by the richness and colour of medieval centuries ; once looked at in and for themselves, these centuries became a source of positive intellectual interest, and not merely of emotional excitement. A cynic might add that the medieval centuries could be contemplated with greater detachment after their practical discomforts had been forgotten, and the ground was no longer cumbered with the debris of medieval institutions and customs which had once served a purpose, but continued to survive only as dangerous anachronisms in a changed political world.

For Germans in particular, the study of the middle ages provided a political as well as a literary inspiration. The medieval empire was the archetype of German unity, and, it might be added, of German secular domination over large areas of Europe. What Germans had once achieved, they could achieve again ; German superiority, lost or submerged in the political and religious wars after the reformation, might be reasserted. There were no such political motives in Great Britain, where the antiquarian scholarship of three centuries had failed to arouse

37

more than a faint interest in medieval history. Sir Walter Scott touched the work of these antiquaries with his genius, but the study of medieval history on the grand scale was not undertaken in Great Britain until the Germans had transformed the character of historical work in every field.

During the nineteenth century it was indeed customary to exaggerate the uniqueness of German scholarship. The authority of Lord Acton has been given to the view that England had nothing to teach Germany, and Germans everything to teach Englishmen in historical method. Acton went to Germany as a young man at a time when the German schools of history were at the height of their fame. He knew little about the detailed work done by the English antiquaries, and to his death, never realised the value of this work in departments of knowledge to which, in spite of his vast learning, he was a stranger.

Nevertheless Acton was right in the sense that the gap between the antiquaries and the historians in Great Britain was not bridged in the early nineteenth century, and that the English historians of this time learned most of their critical methods from Germany. They might have learned these methods from France, where the foundation of the Ecole des Chartes in 1821 continued in secular hands the splendid traditions of scholarship set by the French Benedictines of the eighteenth century. The generation in England which followed the Napoleonic wars was, however, readier to take lessons from Germans than from Frenchmen.

The slowness with which educated opinion in Great Britain demanded the highest standards in historical methods can be seen in the history of the keeping of the national records. A Record Commission was created in London as early as 1801, a quarter of a century before the appearance of the German collection *Monumenta Germaniae historica*. The Commission was filled with important personages who knew nothing about the editing of documents. Neither the Society of Antiquaries nor the universities interested themselves in the matter; hence little good work was done until, in 1830, Harris Nicolas, the editor of Nelson's letters, published a protest against the carelessness with which the records were treated. After the Reform Act of 1832 there was a change for the better. The Public Record Office was established in 1838; a new Record Commission which included experts, began a series of publications *in extenso* or in the form of abridgements or "calendars." The appointment of a Historical Manuscripts Commission in 1869 has led to similar provision for the care of manuscripts in private hands.

Meanwhile, and again outside the universities, English writers had begun to apply the new apparatus of scholarship to historical work intended for an ever widening public. Lingard's *History of England*, the first of these new books, began to appear in 1819. Lingard was a Catholic priest whose purpose in writing was to convince Englishmen, by a careful exposition of historical fact, that they held wrong views about the Catholic Church. He pleased neither Catholic nor Protestant controversialists, but the quietness, honesty, and high competence of his work gave it a place which it kept throughout the greater part of last century as a standard general history.

'THE DEATH OF WOLFE'
Engraving after the painting by Benjamin West, 1771

For some time after the appearance of Lingard's first volume the new interpretation of ancient history begun by Niebuhr (a Holsteiner who took service in
Prussia) became the main interest of a generation of Englishmen trained in classical
scholarship. Arnold's *History of Rome* and Thirlwall's *History of Greece* were written under this influence ; Grote also acknowledged the "inestimable aid of German
erudition." Grote's *History of Greece*, which eclipsed Thirlwall's book in popularity, is of particular interest as the only historical work of importance (other than
James Mill's *History of India under British Rule*) produced by the English philosophical radicals of the early nineteenth century. Arnold and Thirlwall were men
of strong personality and strong political views, but they kept their politics out of
sight in their histories. Grote never concealed his intention of writing a defence of
Greek democracy ; the defence might have been more satisfactory if it had been
based upon a real understanding of the fundamental differences between demo-
cratic government in the ancient and modern worlds. Grote was a learned but not
an interesting historian ; it is not easy to account for the popularity of his book over
many years except on the simple (though remarkable) ground that, since Grote's
time, no English historian has attempted a full-length general history of the great
age of Greece.

X

GROTE'S political bias takes on a mild appearance before the cocksureness of Hallam and Macaulay. On the whole Hallam was more imperturbably certain of himself. Macaulay could monopolise a conversation by sheer brilliance ; a friend once described Hallam as a "perfect boa-contradictor in argument." It is also doubtful whether Macaulay ever committed himself to a judgment as sublime as Hallam's assertion that the whigs had "a natural tendency to political improvement, the tories a natural aversion to it." Hallam's *Constitutional History of England from the accession of Henry VII to the death of George II* was written on this thesis. Hallam has been called a hanging judge ; his verdicts are usually too severe and often deserve the attacks which Southey made on them in the *Quarterly Review*. Moreover, although he took the greatest pains over his work, Hallam was not a scholar in the sense in which Palgrave or von Ranke were scholars. Modern research has upset a good deal of the evidence upon which his over-confident interpretations were based.

Hallam's influence was very great, and, for a circle of readers whose taste was not over-exacting and to whom boredom came less easily than to Lord Bolingbroke, the *Constitutional History* was an ideal exposition of a polity in which freedom slowly broadened down from precedent to precedent, and did not broaden too far or too fast. There is some charm in the fact that this heavy-handed work, which Queen Elizabeth would have torn up in anger and Charles II would have thrown away out of *ennui*, was studied with earnestness by the youthful Victoria and Albert.

If Macaulay was less "goddam" about the whigs as such, he was even more satisfied with his own age. It is therefore easy to call him a "cultured philistine." It is easier and sillier to say that he was merely a *bourgeois* writing for *bourgeois*. In 1848, after the publication of the first and second volumes of his history, Macaulay received a vote of thanks from a working men's club for "having written a history which working men can understand." The late Sir Charles Firth, in his excellent *Commentary on Macaulay's History,* said the same thing from a different angle : "Macaulay never wrote an obscure sentence in his life, and this may seem a very small merit unless we remember of how few writers we could say the same." Macaulay himself is even more illuminating about his style : "My manner is, I think, and the world thinks, on the whole a good one ; but it is very near to a bad manner indeed, and those characteristics of my style which are most easily copied are the most questionable."

Carlyle, who "did not much like happy men," made the absurd comment that "four hundred editions of the *History*" could not lend it any permanent value. Macaulay had obvious limitations. He was not a deep thinker ; like Gibbon, he failed to understand the significance of many of the noblest activities of mankind. As a writer, he had an astonishing power of description, but little sense of design. The scale upon which he began to write a history of England from the Restoration to the death of George IV might well have been too large for any man ; too large

THOMAS CARLYLE 1795–1881

Oil painting by J. McNeil Whistler

E. A. FREEMAN 1823-1892

Oil painting by Hubert Vos, 1889

perhaps, even for a man of Macaulay's genius who had been free to give the greater part of his life to study. Macaulay was forty-eight in the year in which the *History* began to appear. He had been called to the Bar in 1826 and had already started his long series of essays for the *Edinburgh Review*. He was elected to parliament in 1830 and, in 1833, appointed a member of the Supreme Council of India. He spent three and a half years in India ; during this time he laid the foundations of the Indian educational system and composed, almost single-handed, codes of criminal law and criminal procedure. He continued to sit in parliament on his return to England and for a time held office. Macaulay had talked in "printed words" from the age of three, yet, with his many interests, and with a liking for ordinary social life, the task of reading all the material for his subject was overwhelming. In spite of these difficulties Macaulay finished his third and fourth volumes. If he had lived fifteen years longer, he might have achieved the impossible, and completed at least half of his task.

The catalogue of Macaulay's faults might be extended. In a final count they would be reckoned as light weight in comparison with his immense and solid genius. He was master of the first-hand authorities which he used. He made fewer mistakes of detail in a volume than many of his critics in a single chapter. Dislike of his robustness is sometimes a sign of weakness of nerve on the part of his readers. Macaulay was not necessarily wrong because he believed in whig principles ; few people who know the facts would question his assumption that, for ninety out of a hundred of the inhabitants of Great Britain, the early Victorian age was a better time than the reigns of James II or William and Mary. As for Macaulay's "lack of elevation," human life is lived, and may be studied, at different levels. Macaulay never claimed to write the history of thought or action at the highest levels, but this does not mean that all history should be written as from the mountain tops, or that Macaulay is necessarily superficial because he did not see England in the age of the Revolution *sub specie aeternitatis* as Wordsworth once saw London from Westminster Bridge.

For different reasons Carlyle may also be called a great historian. Carlyle shared with Macaulay, and indeed with all historians of genius, the power of losing himself in his work until, in the paradox of artistic creation, the work became impersonal and universal. Take, for example, Carlyle's account of the night before the battle of Dunbar :

> "And so the soldiers stand to their arms, or lie within reach of their arms all night. . . The night is wild and wet ; 2nd September meaning 12th by our calendar ; the Harvest Moon wades deep among clouds of sleet and hail. Whoever hath a heart for prayer, let him pray now, for the wrestle of death is at hand. Thus they pass the night. . . We English have some tents ; the Scots have none. The hoarse sea moans bodeful, swinging low and heavy against whinstone bays ; the sea and the tempests are abroad ; all else asleep but we—and there is one that rides on the wings of the wind."

This paragraph breaks all the rules of prose rhythm and composition which lesser writers, if they are prudent, will take care to observe. In any case it is an odd paragraph to find in an edition of a historical text. Yet there must be thousands of

Englishmen who, like myself, came upon it in boyhood, and ever afterwards, at sight of the harvest moon, think of Cromwell's army on a wild September night in 1650.

Carlyle did not begin to write history until his fortieth year. Perhaps he never wrote history ; the *French Revolution* is nearer to Hardy's *Dynasts* than to a prose record of political events. Carlyle, in fact, did not care much for "policy." He was interested in people and, above all, in problems of right and wrong ; so much interested in right and wrong and in the assertion of personality that he began to confuse power with right. His book on Frederick the Great suffered from this confusion and therefore exasperates modern English readers. For all his recklessness of judgment Carlyle took immense pains over his work. He was never "ravenous" for facts ; he admitted, or rather, declaimed, that the duty of reading masses of inartistic material was a weariness. He described the sources for the Cromwellian period as "a waste continent of cinders" and the German historians of Frederick as "dark, chaotic dullards." In spite of all, he found his way through cinder heaps and chaos, and gave an interpretation which needs correction in detail but is still valid in the large both for Cromwell and for many of the chief actors of the French Revolution.

XI

THE careers of four men, Freeman, Froude, Green, and Stubbs, who dominate English historical writing for a generation after 1860, shew the transition to the modern age of the professional or "professorial" historian. Although three of the four held the Regius chair at Oxford, their main work was done elsewhere, and they learned little of historical method from the university. Freeman's *History of the Norman Conquest* loses nothing as a story from his enthusiasm for the Anglo-Saxons. On the other hand his interpretation of the Conquest was defective because he worked almost entirely upon printed records which he could use in his Somerset country house.

Froude also did most of his writing at country houses in Wales and Devonshire, but he armed himself with material from Spanish as well as English archives. Froude wrote at even greater length than Freeman ; his *History of England from the Fall of Wolsey to the Defeat of the Spanish Armada* fills twelve volumes. These volumes were bitterly attacked. To some extent Froude laid himself open to severe criticism. Newman and Carlyle, the two main influences in Froude's life, hardly set him examples of steadiness of opinion or of judgments unclouded by emotion. Froude's later friendship with Kingsley (whose sister-in-law he married) did little to correct his faults. His critics accused him of gross carelessness as well as of bias. In some respects Froude was careless, but he was compelled to do much of his archival research in circumstances which made accurate copying almost impossible. It may be said that he has cleared himself of the most damaging "technical" charges. His bias is beyond defence. His interpretation of documents, his likes and dislikes, or rather, his loves and hates are often absurd. The late Sir Adolphus Ward once pointed out that the "list of animals to whom Mary, Queen of Scots, is in turn com-

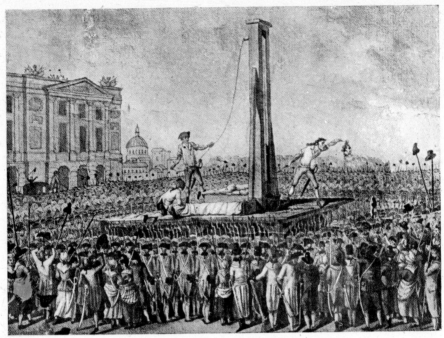

'THE TRAGIC END OF LOUIS XVI, 1793'
Water colour by a contemporary artist

pared in Froude's History is that of a small menagerie.'' This wilfulness in painting heroes or villains according to his tastes has lost Froude a position to which otherwise he is fully entitled. His work might have been a classic for generations, if his readers had not been left to wonder all the time whether they were not following a *tour de force* of the most sustained and magnificent kind.

The readers of Stubbs' sober and learned pages are spared any such doubts. Although Stubbs saw the middle ages through the distorting atmosphere of his own time, he was never a partisan. His scholarship was rather of the magisterial kind which deserves and obtains confidence. Stubbs learned Anglo-Saxon at school and began to read medieval documents in the court house of his native town of Knaresborough. The greatest of his books, the *Constitutional History of England*, was published between 1873 and 1878 ; that is to say, after he had done much work in editing the Rolls series of English chronicles, and before his time was occupied by the administration of the large diocese of Oxford. Stubbs wrote for scholars and students and, for them, he remains a master. He set the lines of research for half a century ; even to-day no one would think of attempting serious investigation into the medieval history of England without first reading everything which Stubbs has written on the subject.

J. R. GREEN, 1837-1883
Engraving by G. J. Stodart from a chalk drawing by F. Sandys

John Richard Green was less epic in style than Freeman and less dispassionate in manner than Stubbs, though both Freeman and Stubbs admired his work, and did their best to help him. Freeman, in fact, put all his rough energy into the support of "Johnny Green." Green did not need much "boost." His *Short History of the English People* (1874) was an immediate success. The title was as fortunate as the date of publication. In the period between the second and third reform acts of the nineteenth century, and a few years after the passing of Forster's Education Act, there was a public waiting for a history, not of the English kings, but of the commons of the realm. Green's title was not, however, just a bait ; the public was given a work of art. Green had been a clergyman in the East end of London from 1860 to 1869 ; he had written a number of "middles" for the *Saturday Review*, mainly on historical subjects. He left his parish in 1869 for the librarianship of Lambeth (a post from which many contributions of value have been made to English historical studies) at a time when he was threatened with consumption. Green died at Menton in his forty-sixth year ; before his death he had written a longer version of his *Short History*. The longer version was not better than the earlier work, and it is doubtful whether Green could have improved on it. The *Short History* owed much of its vividness to the rare conjuncture of knowledge and emotion under which it was written. The book was Green's protest against the drabness and poverty of

Victorian London; a historian's protest, as William Morris's *Dream of John Ball* was the protest of a master-craftsman. The book was thus the first of its kind in England (Carlyle's *Past and Present* was more of a pamphlet than a history) to be written under the influence of a new and wider conception of social justice. Arnold Toynbee's *Lectures on the Industrial Revolution* (1884) were written from a similar impulse. The two books shew the change in opinion since Hallam and Macaulay; a change which has led, in our own time, and again following the demand of a new class of reader, to the close and specialised study of economic history. This study had indeed begun from the side of the economists and statisticians before the "political" historians paid detailed attention to it. The first two volumes of J. E. Thorold Rogers' *History of Agriculture and Prices* appeared in 1866 ; a generation earlier J. R. Porter's *Progress of the Nation* had shewn the difference between the new "statistical approach" and the itineraries and surveys of the age of Leland and Stow, or even of the period of Arthur Young.

The other historians of this remarkable age of scholarship and writing also bring one to the eve of the twentieth century. Lecky's greatest work, *A History of England in the Eighteenth Century* (1878-90), was written in a colder mood than Green's *Short History*, but once again the book shews in a curious way the turn in interest towards the history of ideas and of social and economic movements, and the mood of opinion in Great Britain during this long age of peace ; it is almost impossible to imagine that a German historian, writing within a decade after Bismarck's three wars, would have dismissed the battle of Blenheim in a sentence. On the other hand, Lecky's book is, like Spencer Walpole's *History of Twenty-Five Years*, a record of change for the better ; greater liberty of mind, a softening of manners, a more sensitive public conscience.

Lecky and Walpole were interested mainly in the British Isles, or at all events, in the development of civilisation in Europe. Seeley was the first English historian to feel something of Hakluyt's exultation in the majesty of English power. Seeley's *Expansion of England in the Eighteenth Century* belongs to the new age of imperialism. In some measure Seeley's enthusiasm was unfortunate. He was too didactic and too much of a partisan to be the founder of a school of historians of the British Empire. Hence the subject was neglected for several decades, and has not been rescued until our own time from political controversy. One branch indeed has never been treated satisfactorily ; since Mill's time no history of India under British rule (with the exception of Lyall's *Rise and Expansion of the British dominion in India*) has done justice to the interest of the subject.

XII

THE foundation of the *English Historical Review* in, 1886 with Creighton as editor, may be taken as the beginning of the modern epoch in which short historical studies of the first rank have ceased to find a place in quarterly or monthly journals, and the accumulation and specialised treatment of historical material have set almost as many problems as they have solved. Freeman once complained that "history has no technical terms" to frighten incompetent writers from writing historical books. In the twentieth century one might complain that history has too may technical terms, and that the old gap between the antiquaries and the historians has widened again after a recession in the mid-Victorian era.

The gap has become wider in many respects. It is wider in life as well as in learning. With the increased *tempo* of social and political change, and with the rapid movement of the population, the average man—now a townsman—tends to be a *déraciné*, cut off from the past of his own people and country. Few people in the large cities of England even know where their great-grandparents are buried. It is harder to visualise the past when you do not live in it as the English and Scots of earlier centuries lived among institutions of church and state which linked together the generations. In the sphere of learning, the problem is equally difficult. As more is known about earlier periods, the "marginal area" of knowledge, upon which research tends to be concentrated, becomes withdrawn from the field of vision of the ordinary reader. A detailed investigation into the economic life of the fifteenth century or into the finances of the Stuart kings is bound to involve terms and assumptions with which experts alone are familiar. Fifty years ago F. W. Maitland wrote on the history of English law and institutions with great brilliance and lucidity, yet it is not easy for a layman to follow Maitland's arguments, or to realise the full significance of his work in the interpretation of medieval England. The real question, however, is not whether all historical work is of equal interest or even of equal intelligibility to the public at large. The public is interested in the results, not in the processes of the ascertainment of significant fact. There have been historians in recent times (the late Professor Bury of Cambridge was one of them) who have been ready, in theory, though not in their own work, to allow history to become an esoteric science. The wisest contemporary historians have refused to accept this view. Sir Charles Firth was by common consent, one of the most learned men of his time. He was also one of the most accomplished and interesting writers. In his *Commentary on Macaulay's History*, Firth discussed Bury's view that "to clothe the story of human society in a literary dress is not more the part of a historian as an historian, than it is the part of an astronomer to present in an artistic shape the story of the stars." Firth's comment was given with his usual Yorkshire good sense : "After all, when a man puts his pen to paper and proceeds to print the result, he is attempting to convey his ideas to some other man. He presupposes the existence of a reader. It is therefore essential that he should arrange his ideas clearly, that he should state them so that they may be understood, and express them so that they may leave a lasting impression on the mind of the person to whom they are addressed. If he fails to achieve this, he has done only half of his work."

It would be invidious to attempt an inclusive list of names as evidence that most "professorial" historians of to-day agree with Sir Charles Firth, but one might take three examples as typical of the scholarship of three universities of Oxford, Cambridge, and London : Pollard's *Henry VIII*, Trevelyan's *England under Queen Anne*, and Powicke's *The Christian Life in the Middle Ages*. Furthermore, the historians of our own time have not only known how to combine good scholarship with good

J. A. FROUDE 1818-1894
Chalk drawing by Samuel Lawrence, 1863

writing; they have also done much to develop a technique of co-operative work which goes a long way towards solving the problem of the isolation of the specialist in his separate sphere. The progress made during the last thirty years in the co-ordination of the work of individual scholars may be seen by a comparison between the earliest and the latest of the Cambridge series of general histories.

One might also notice that, since 1914, British historians have realised more clearly that the writing of history need not be confined to the remoter centuries.

There has indeed been a return to the seventeenth-century fashion of writing contemporary history. This revival of interest in the day before yesterday has been due partly to demands made upon historians by the public. The historians have been able to meet the demand because to-day there is much greater material than a hundred years ago for writing the history of the immediate past on a scientific basis. In the seventeenth century "conversation and familiarity in the inside of courts" were necessary for a historian who wished to write a history of his own time ; to-day there are few aspects of recent history outside the sphere of foreign policy which are not fully documented. The greater part of the material for the study of social and economic history is to be found in sources available to students within a year or two of the events concerned.

Historians in the last two decades have been set more difficult problems than the elucidation of events which are still within living memory. The reading public asks for a final interpretation of history, and for an answer to the question why civilisations rise and fall. Is there, as Hume thought, a tidal movement in human affairs and nothing more than this tidal ebb and flow ? Is there no hope of stability or of unmixed achievement in the temporal sphere or can it be said that, in spite of ages of regression towards barbarism, historians are able to bring evidence of progress towards a desirable end ?

To these questions British historians are not very ready to give an answer, and, in general, the answers which are given are not put forward by the most learned or the most profound scholars. In the preface to his *History of Europe* H. A. L. Fisher wrote that he had no ultimate philosophy of history. Such a view does not imply scepticism, or even lack of belief in the possibility of a final synthesis. The difficulty at present is that the *data* are insufficient. To a historian the history of the world of man is a very short history. The years of the astronomers and the geologists reach beyond a historian's reckoning ; a small fraction only of these vast epochs is covered by the period during which man, with knowledge of the wheel, of fire, of pottery, and of edged tools, has set out to be master of his environment. Within this fragment of time, the history of lettered and civilised man fills an even smaller space. It is therefore not remarkable that a satisfactory clue has yet to be found to the meaning of the strange acts of the strangest of living creatures. Bede tells the story of the Northumbrian thane who compared the life of man on earth, in relation to the unknown immensity of time, to a moment in which a bird might fly into the warmth of a hall in winter, and then be lost to sight again in the storms—*de hieme in hiemem regrediens*. Of this short space of time men had knowledge ; they knew nothing of what had gone before, nothing of what might follow after.

British historians are not necessarily without "the care of knowing causes" if they refuse to commit themselves to any more definite judgment upon the pattern of history and the meaning of human existence.